Endorsements for the Flourish Bible Study Series

"The brilliant and beautiful mix of sound teaching, helpful charts, lists, sidebars, and appealing graphics—as well as insightful questions that get the reader into the text of Scripture—makes these studies that women will want to invest time in and will look back on as time well spent."
Nancy Guthrie, Bible teacher; author, *Even Better than Eden*

"My daughter and I love using Flourish Bible Studies for our morning devotions. Lydia Brownback's faithful probing of biblical texts; insightful questions; invitations to engage in personal applications using additional biblical texts and historical contexts; and commitment to upholding the whole counsel of God as it bears on living life as a godly woman have drawn us closer to the Lord and to his word. Brownback never sidesteps hard questions or hard providences, but neither does she appeal to discourses of victimhood or therapy, which are painfully common in the genre of women's Bible studies. I cannot recommend this series highly enough. My daughter and I look forward to working through this whole series together!"
Rosaria Butterfield, Former Professor of English, Syracuse University; author, *The Gospel Comes with a House Key*

"As a women's ministry leader, I am excited about the development of the Flourish Bible Study series, which will not only prayerfully equip women to increase in biblical literacy but also come alongside them to build a systematic and comprehensive framework to become lifelong students of the word of God. This series provides visually engaging studies with accessible content that will not only strengthen the believer but the church as well."
Karen Hodge, Coordinator of Women's Ministries, Presbyterian Church in America; coauthor, *Transformed*

"Lydia Brownback is an experienced Bible teacher who has dedicated her life to ministry roles that help women (and men) grow in Christ. With a wealth of biblical, historical, and theological content, her Flourish Bible Studies are ideal for groups and individuals that are serious about the in-depth study of the word of God."
Phil and Lisa Ryken, President, Wheaton College; and his wife, Lisa

"If you're looking for rich, accessible, and deeply biblical Bible studies, this series is for you! Lydia Brownback leads her readers through different books of the Bible, providing background information, maps, timelines, and questions that probe the text in order to glean understanding and application. She settles us deeply in the context of a book as she highlights God's unfolding plan of redemption and rescue. You will learn, you will delight in God's word, and you will love our good King Jesus even more."
Courtney Doctor, Coordinator of Women's Initiatives, The Gospel Coalition; author, *From Garden to Glory* and *Steadfast*

"Lydia Brownback's Bible study series provides a faithful guide to book after book. You'll find rich insights into context and good questions to help you study and interpret the Bible. Page by page, the studies point you to respond to each passage and to love our great and gracious God. I will recommend the Flourish series for years to come for those looking for a wise, Christ-centered study that leads toward the goal of being transformed by the word."

Taylor Turkington, Bible teacher; Director, BibleEquipping.org

"Lydia Brownback has a contagious love for the Bible. Not only is she fluent in the best of biblical scholarship in the last generation, but her writing is accessible to the simplest of readers. She has the rare ability of being clear without being reductionistic. I anticipate many women indeed will flourish through her trustworthy guidance in this series."

David Mathis, Senior Teacher and Executive Editor, desiringGod.org; Pastor, Cities Church, Saint Paul, Minnesota; author, *Habits of Grace*

"Lydia Brownback's Flourish Bible Study series has been a huge gift to the women's ministry in my local church. Many of our groups have gone through her studies in both the Old and New Testaments and have benefited greatly. The Flourish Bible Study series is now my go-to for a combination of rich Bible study, meaningful personal application, and practical group interaction. I recommend them whenever a partner in ministry asks me for quality women's Bible study resources. I'm so thankful Brownback continues to write them and share them with us!"

Jen Oshman, author, *Enough about Me* and *Cultural Counterfeits*; Women's Ministry Coordinator, Redemption Parker, Colorado

JOB

Flourish Bible Study Series
By Lydia Brownback

Judges: The Path from Chaos to Kingship

Esther: The Hidden Hand of God

Job: Trusting God When Suffering Comes

Habakkuk: Learning to Live by Faith

Luke: Good News of Great Joy

Philippians: Living for Christ

James: Walking in Wisdom

1–2 Peter: Living Hope in a Hard World

FLOURISH
BIBLE STUDY

JOB

TRUSTING GOD WHEN SUFFERING COMES

LYDIA BROWNBACK

WHEATON, ILLINOIS

Crossway is a publishing ministry of Good News Publishers.

RRDS		34	33	32	31	30	29	28	27	26	25	24
14	13	12	11	10	9	8	7	6	5	4	3	2

To my precious mother,
Wilma Lorraine Grunert Brownback,
whose faith never wavers.

"For I know that my Redeemer lives,
and at the last he will stand upon the earth."
Job 19:25

CONTENTS

THE PLACE OF JOB
IN BIBLICAL HISTORY

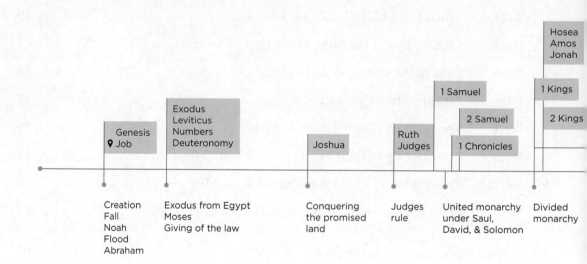

Genesis ♥ Job	Exodus Leviticus Numbers Deuteronomy	Joshua	Ruth Judges	1 Samuel 2 Samuel 1 Chronicles	Hosea Amos Jonah 1 Kings 2 Kings

Creation
Fall
Noah
Flood
Abraham

Exodus from Egypt
Moses
Giving of the law

Conquering
the promised
land

Judges
rule

United monarchy
under Saul,
David, & Solomon

Divided
monarchy

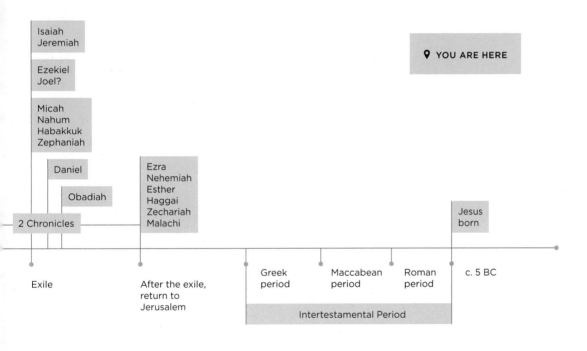

Isaiah
Jeremiah

Ezekiel
Joel?

Micah
Nahum
Habakkuk
Zephaniah

Daniel

Obadiah

Ezra
Nehemiah
Esther
Haggai
Zechariah
Malachi

2 Chronicles

Jesus
born

📍 YOU ARE HERE

Exile

After the exile,
return to
Jerusalem

Greek
period

Maccabean
period

Roman
period

c. 5 BC

Intertestamental Period

INTRODUCTION

GETTING INTO JOB

Why? There comes a time when each one of us asks that *why* question in bewildered, heart-searing pain. And it's a cry to God alone, because only he knows the answer. When a child dies or a husband betrays or a malignancy forms, we want answers. Have we done something to cause it? Is the Lord angry with us? Why does he seem so distant and uncaring? And in the darkness of what feels like divine indifference, we find ourselves questioning his power, his goodness, and his love. That's what happened to Job. He was a man who suffered the loss of everything he had—family, home, wealth, friends, success, prosperity, and health. But worst of all, God seemed indifferent. Some friends came to comfort Job, but they were unable to help him, and in fact, they only intensified his pain. In time, Job's suffering did end, and his losses were restored, but not until the Lord spoke to Job and radically changed his heart. From Job we learn that whatever we suffer, God is in control. And he is up to something good.

WHO'S WHO IN JOB

First we meet Job, of course. He was a prosperous farmer and a family man who worshiped God. Job was highly respected far and wide not only for his prosperity but also for his integrity. There's also Satan, an adversarial being who opposes God and everything in God's creation, especially human beings. Other key figures in the story are Job's three friends Eliphaz, Bildad, and Zophar. Later we meet a man named Elihu, a young friend who turns out to be wiser than Job's three older friends. Unnamed but everywhere in the story is the narrator, the one behind the scenes recounting all that happens to Job. We gather that the narrator lived a long time after the story takes place—his grasp of God's words and ways were not yet known in Job's lifetime but only much later. Finally, as we near the end of the story, the Lord reveals himself in all his power and majesty. The book of Job is primarily about him, the Lord of heaven and earth.

Pronunciation Guide

Job: Jobe   **Eliphaz:** EL-la-faz   **Zophar:** ZO-far

Bildad: BILL-dad   **Behemoth:** Ba-HEEM-oth

Elihu: Ah-LEE-hoo   **Leviathan:** Lev-EYE-ah-thon

SETTING

Job lived in Uz. Bible scholars aren't sure exactly where Uz was, but they are confident that this territory was not within Canaan, the land God promised to give to his people Israel. Uz might have been situated in the land of Edom. Most likely Job lived around the same time as one of the patriarchs—Abraham, Isaac, or Jacob—who are found in the first book of the Bible, Genesis.

THEMES

Suffering is the primary theme in Job, especially suffering that seems to make no sense. In keeping with this theme, we are given a behind-the-scenes glimpse into the spiritual realm and how it factors into suffering. As we follow Job through his pain, we learn how to think about God in the midst of overwhelming difficulty—how to understand and trust him. The book of Job also shows how we can help (or harm) a suffering friend. Overarching all of these themes is what the book of Job reveals about the Lord himself—his power, wisdom, and authority over everything, including evil.

"Job is about true worship, a person bowing down in the darkness to the one who is God, leaving even our most agonized unanswered questions at his feet."[1]

STUDYING JOB

During this ten-week study, we will read all forty-two chapters of Job. The reading is not spread out evenly over the ten weeks, so you'll find that some weeks necessitate a good bit more reading than others. Typically you'll want to read a week's entire passage before doing the lesson, but you might want to approach the Bible reading in this study on a "read as you go," section-by-section basis. If you are studying Job with a group, you can read select portions aloud together when you gather together. However you approach the reading, remember that *marinating in the Scripture text is the most important part of any Bible study.*

GROUP STUDY

If you are doing this study as part of a group, you'll want to finish each week's lesson before the group meeting. You can work your way through the study questions all in one sitting or by doing a little bit each day. And don't be discouraged if you don't have sufficient time to answer every question. Just do as much as you can, knowing that the more you do, the more you'll learn. No matter how much of the study you are able to complete each week, the group will benefit simply from your presence, so don't skip the gathering if you can't finish! That being said, group time will be most rewarding for every participant if you have done the lesson in advance.

If you are leading the group, you can download the leaders' tips at https://www.lydiabrownback.com/flourish-series.

INDIVIDUAL STUDY

The study is designed to run for ten weeks, but you can set your own pace if you're studying solo. And you can download the leaders' tips (https://www.lydiabrownback.com/flourish-series) if you'd like some guidance along the way.

Marinating in the Scripture text is the most important part of any Bible study

Reading Plan

	Primary Text	Supplemental Reading
Week 1	Job 1:1–2:13	Jude 24
Week 2	Job 3:1–26	Psalm 88
Week 3	Job 4:1–14:22	
Week 4	Job 15:1–21:34	
Week 5	Job 22:1–27:23	
Week 6	Job 28:1–28	Proverbs 2:1–4
Week 7	Job 29:1–31:40	
Week 8	Job 32:1–37:24	
Week 9	Job 38:1–41:34	
Week 10	Job 42:1–17	James 5:11

A SHATTERED LIFE

JOB 1:1-2:13

Norah was voted "most popular" her senior year of high school. Four years later she graduated college with a near-perfect GPA, three job offers, and a marriage proposal from Lucas, the football MVP and class valedictorian. She chose marriage and settled with her new husband into a large suburban home set back on a tree-lined street. His career success kept pace with the growth of their family—three children in five years. In the midst of it all, the young family took an active role in church life because they loved the Lord. Norah was a sought-after friend known for her listening ear, compassionate heart, and life-of-the-party personality. People flocked to Norah in hopes that her charmed life might rub off on them. What had she done to get so blessed? Was it her kindness or her faithfulness at church or choosing to be a stay-at-home mom? They stopped wondering a year later when Norah's life fell apart. On a dark November night, Lucas was killed by a drunk driver, leaving Norah a single mother with three kids and another on the way.

It's tempting to think that personal prosperity is a sign of God's favor, isn't it? The reverse is also true—we can find ourselves hunting for a direct link between suffering and sin. But stories like Norah's debunk those ideas. The answers we need for stories like Norah's are found in the Bible, and that's where we encounter Job, a godly man who suffered the loss of absolutely everything he had. This week we are given a glimpse into the secret happenings in heaven, and it's there we find out something that Job wanted desperately to know—a reason for his suffering.

1. A FAMILY MAN (1:1–5)

When the story opens, Job is living the sort of life everyone dreams of. By worldly standards, he had it all.

Four traits are attributed to Job in verse 1: (1) he is blameless; (2) he is upright; (3) he fears God; and (4) he turns away from evil. In case you were wondering, "blameless" certainly doesn't mean *sinless*, as we will see. The Hebrew word that our Bibles translate as "blameless" has to do with integrity and transparency. You also might wonder about Job's fear—he feared God. But this fear isn't about terror or stressful anxiety. It has to do with reverence and respect. Job lived his life with an eye to pleasing God in everything.

✦ Based on the way Job is described in verse 1, summarize his character in a sentence or two, using your own words.

> ### Satan
>
> "Satan's origins are mysterious. . . . At times, this spiritual being of immense power and cunning works his mischief as an angel of light. Other times he is like a ravenous lion on the prowl. He is a spoiler. He is a disuniter. He is the enemy of the interpersonal. Temptation is his specialty from the beginning. Christians need to have a worldview that takes the devil seriously."[2]

✦ In verses 2–3 we get an idea of the scope of Job's people and possessions. He has seven sons and three daughters as well as seven thousand sheep and three thousand camels. In addition, there are five hundred each of oxen and female donkeys and an enormous staff of servants. The actual numbers are significant. In the Bible, the numbers seven and three often communicate *completion*. And when you add together seven plus three, the number ten that results is also significant. Ten also stands for completeness, or fullness. As you consider the significance of these numbers here in these verses, what do they communicate about Job's life?

We get a glimpse into Job's family life in 1:4–5. They gather for family dinners on special occasions, very likely the sons' birthdays. We also notice that they live in houses rather than tents, which is another indicator of the family's great wealth. After these family gatherings, Job would offer sacrifices for his children, concerned that perhaps they did not reverence God or desire to serve him. Here we see Job's heart for his kids, his fatherly concern for their spiritual welfare. He might be able to provide them with everything on a material level, but when it comes to spiritual matters, he could only petition the Lord.

> *"If we love God only for what he gives us in this life and not for himself, we are serving ourselves, not him."*[3]

2. WHEN SATAN COMES CALLING (1:6–12)

For just a moment, the veil lifts, and we are given a glimpse of things hidden. In this case, it's a gathering of the divine council—a group of heavenly beings centered on the Lord God. Into this gathering comes a being called Satan. From the way his entrance is described here, he doesn't seem to be a part of the council. He's more of a gate-crasher. The term *satan* means "adversary," and the word was used not only for this particular being but for adversaries of all kinds. The being who appears here, though, carries the term *satan* as a title. He is actually not just Satan, but *the* Satan.

✦ As Satan enters the council, who initiates the conversation about Job?

✦ What does Satan suggest about Job in 1:9–12?

....

....

....

....

Satan claims that the Lord has put a hedge around Job's life (v. 10). The hedge concerned Job's prosperity, the Lord's protection over Job's farm and his wealth and his family. The hedge image is a way of talking about how the Lord guides, guards, and directs everything that happens in the lives of people.

✦ The Lord's hedge of protection around Job and all that was dear to him is a picture of much fuller hedges of protection that the Lord puts around his people. What do we learn about these fuller *hedges* from the following passages?

   · Luke 22:31–32

....

....

....

   · John 10:28–29

....

....

....

   · Romans 8:38–39

....

....

....

· Jude 24

✦ What does the Lord permit Satan to do in 1:12, and what does he forbid?

3. WIPED OUT (1:13-22)

Job's life changes in a matter of minutes when four messengers come, one at a time, each with terrible news.

✦ Jot down in your own words the news each messenger brings:

· Messenger 1:

· Messenger 2:

· Messenger 3:

....

....

....

· Messenger 4:

....

....

....

✦ It's hard to imagine experiencing even one of these losses, much less all four in the same day! When the messengers depart, Job tears his robe and shaves his head—a sign of great grief and mourning—but at the same time, he worships God. What do Job's words in 1:21 reveal about the nature of true faith?

....

....

....

....

4. SKIN FOR SKIN! (2:1–10)

The divine council reconvenes, and once again, Satan shows up and seeks a seat at the table.

✦ What argument does Satan make in 2:4–5?

....

....

....

....

✦ What limits does the Lord set on Satan this go-round?

We don't know how much time has passed since Job's tragic losses. No matter, the pain of those losses is still overwhelming, and now added to his grief is an itchy, painful skin condition. Plus it's clear that Job's wife has had enough. This is the only time she comes into the story, and no doubt her bitter words in 2:9, while certainly understandable, given her own suffering through all these losses, just heap more pain on Job.

✦ How do the words of Job's wife in 2:9 serve to further the agenda of Satan that was revealed in 2:5?

✦ How is what Job's wife does here in 2:9 similar to what Eve, the very first wife, did to her husband back in Genesis 3:1–7? On the other hand, how is Job's response to his wife in 2:10 different from Adam's response to his wife Eve?

5. THE COMFORT OF FRIENDS (2:11-13)

It's not surprising that a man of Job's wealth and success had made connections in places both far and near, and some of those associates had become good friends. Three of those friends, receiving word of Job's great tragedies, come to visit him. Eliphaz comes from Teman, a city in Edom that was known for wisdom (see Jeremiah 49:7). We know very little about the other two friends—Bildad, who came from Shuah, and Zophar from Naamah—except for a few clues based on what is known about their hometowns.

✦ The three friends had a plan for their visit to Job. What was it?

....

....

....

....

✦ Why do you think Job's friends struggled to recognize him at first?

....

....

....

....

✦ How do the friends carry out what they had planned to do during their visit?

....

....

....

....

Much later in the Bible, in the New Testament, someone else suffered while friends sat nearby. It was Jesus. But the suffering of these two was radically different. Jesus suffered not for his own losses but for ours. When sin entered the world back in Genesis 3, human beings lost life—happy, unbroken, eternal fellowship with God—and thereafter faced death and eternal separation from God. Jesus suffered to restore us to the life we lost through sin. So while Job didn't choose to suffer, Jesus did, willingly, for us. The one similarity we're going to see is that both Job and Jesus were let down by their friends.

✦ Read Matthew 26:36–45. How did Jesus's friends actually increase his suffering rather than comfort him in it?

"There is something desperately extreme about Job.
He foreshadows one man whose greatness exceeded
even Job's, whose sufferings took him deeper than
Job, and whose perfect obedience to his Father
was only anticipated in faint outline by Job."[4]

LET'S TALK

1. When Job learned of his great losses, he responded, "Naked I came from my mother's womb, and naked shall I return. The LORD gave, and the LORD has taken away; blessed be the name of the LORD" (1:21). And then when his wife tempted him to renounce God and just die, he said, "You speak as one of the foolish women would speak. Shall we receive good from God, and shall we not receive evil?" (2:10). Describe how your response to past or present suffering is similar to Job's or radically different. What would it take for you to respond like Job?

....

....

....

....

....

2. Job's friends came to sympathize and comfort him. It's exactly what the apostle Paul tells us to do in Romans 12:15: "Rejoice with those who rejoice, weep with those who weep." What might that look like when you approach present sufferers in your own life? If you are suffering, describe how friends could most help you right now.

....

....

....

....

....

....

....

....

JOB'S BITTER LAMENT

JOB 3:1-26

Some of us remember the unique *clickity-clack* of typewriter keys and the accompanying *ding* at the end of a typed line. We less-skilled typists also remember how we couldn't create any sort of document without a bottle of Wite-Out at the ready, the frequent need to disrupt our labors to paint over a typo with the opaque liquid and then wait for it to dry as we did our best to retain our train of thought. How much more productive we became when personal computers hit the market and changed all that! Even so, today's computer keyboards, while much improved, are similar to those old typewriters. But there is an overarching revolutionary change—the "undo" or "delete" key. No more wet, white goo! Now we can backspace and rekey our words in a matter of seconds. So how much more amazing would it be if we had an "undo" key for life? If, when we sin or say something we regret or make an unwise decision, we could simply tap delete . . . delete . . . delete, and voilà—we could simply "retype" that occurrence as we wish.

Job didn't have keyboards of any sort in his day, but he experienced the same longing to undo or delete. In his case, it was his entire existence. His extreme suffering had begun to darken his thoughts. Intense suffering can tempt any of us toward bitterness and even, at times, to wish that our very existence had never begun. This is hard stuff to read—and kind of shocking—especially because we know that Job was a man of faith. But as we persevere with Job through his raw pain, his cries of anguish, we, like Job, are going to come out of it with our own faith strengthened.

> "Lament is a common biblical genre, and its
> presence in Scripture indicates the appropriate
> role of sadness in the believer's life."[5]

1. LIFE UNDONE (3:1–10)

When we left Job at the end of last week, he was sitting on the ground with his three friends Eliphaz, Bildad, and Zophar. They'd come to mourn with him. Seven days have passed, an entire week, but the friends have said nothing. The magnitude of Job's suffering has left them speechless. Finally, Job opens his mouth and begins to pour out his anguish.

✦ As you read the first ten verses of chapter 3, what words do you encounter again and again, and what emotions do these words convey?

....

....

....

....

> "If there really is no hope, there is no point in asking
> 'Why?' . . . And yet Job does ask 'Why?' and he asks
> it repeatedly and energetically. He says he wants
> to die, but his restless words betray him, for they
> point inexorably to life and resurrection."[6]

Job directs his words here to no one in particular—he doesn't seem to be praying, nor is he speaking directly to his friends. He's simply pouring out his heart. So great is Job's suffering that he wishes he'd never been born. He longs to "undo" his very existence.

Where Job Went Wrong

"Job does not curse the Lord or directly charge him with wrongdoing. That does not mean, however, that Job will make it to the end of the story without any failures. Job does finally repent for what he says throughout the book, and [at the end] God does receive this repentance, which indicates that Job is guilty of some kind of sin in his speech. What, then, is Job's sin?

The answer is to be found in that Job's cursing of the day on which he was born is an implicit questioning of divine wisdom. . . .

It is all too easy to slip from an honest and righteous questioning of God's ways to an implicit denial that what He has done is right and good."[7]

Job isn't suffering because he sinned,
but he does sin in his suffering.

✤ Likely adding to his pain are new and gnawing questions about God. If God were truly good, how could he let so much tragedy into Job's life? No doubt these questions only add to his difficulty. As you consider the particular words Job uses to express his desire to undo his life, read Genesis 1:1–27 and identify another reversal he seems to have in mind here, showing just how deep his pain goes.

> ### Sheol
>
> In the Old Testament, sheol is where the dead reside. Believers find rest in sheol, but for the wicked, it is a place of punishment.[8]

*"Desperation is the denial of hope. Hope looks
forward; desperation can only relive the past
and seek to rewrite it, or even to erase it."*[9]

2. CRAVING REST (3:11–19)

Job continues his lament, noting that he'd be free from pain now if he'd been still-born rather than nurtured by his mother.

✦ Again in verses 11–19 we find repeated words and images that convey how Job is feeling. What do these words add to our understanding about the state of Job's mind and heart?

_____

_____

_____

_____

✦ Job is given no answers to the questions he raises in verses 11–12, which only adds to his troubled state and makes him fantasize about life in sheol, the place of the dead. Who does Job see in sheol, and what is life like there?

_____

_____

_____

_____

✦ What about Job's sheol fantasy—who's there and what goes on—do you think he finds so appealing?

3. CRAVING DARKNESS (3:20–26)

In this final section of Job's lament, we see some light, but it's unwelcome light, so far as Job is concerned. Up until now, there's been nothing but darkness, so we'd expect that light would be a welcome change. But for Job, the light, which is necessary for life, isn't positive.

✦ Job describes himself as "bitter in soul" (v. 20), which indicates something beyond grief. How would you explain what it means to be bitter in soul? You might want to read 1 Samuel 1:1–19, where Hannah experiences this emotion.

✦ Before Job's terrible losses, back when Satan and the Lord had discussed Job during the divine council meeting, Satan had argued that the only reason Job was a righteous man was that God had surrounded him with a "hedge" of blessing (see 1:10). Here in 3:23 we see how the Lord *hedges* people in a different way. Why do you think Job describes himself as "hedged in"?

✦ Job laments, "The thing that I fear comes upon me, and what I dread befalls me" (v. 25). Before Job's life fell apart, we were given a glimpse into what made him anxious. Review 1:4–5 and then note what might be upsetting Job so much here in 3:25.

....

....

....

....

✦ Job's initial lament here in chapter 3 doesn't have a happy ending. This is just one of the ways that Psalm 88 is similar to Job's lament here. Read Psalm 88 and note some similarities to Job's lament.

....

....

....

....

Job has had time to absorb all his losses, and the impact on him seems to have crushed his spirit. Has he lost his faith? After Job lost his livelihood and his children, he'd responded, "The LORD gave, and the LORD has taken away; blessed be the name of the LORD" (1:21). Then when his illness broke out and his wife encouraged him to end his life, he rebuked her and said, "Shall we receive good from God, and shall we not receive evil?" (2:10). Now, it seems, he's doing the very opposite—refusing to accept his losses and wishing to end his life. The story isn't over, of course, but even at this point, we can gain a bit of wisdom from Job's various responses to pain. From him we learn that committed believers can go through some very dark seasons. In other words, his lament in chapter 3 doesn't cancel out his earlier, more positive responses.

✦ Despite the darkness of chapter 3, there's hope hidden here deep in Job's heart. Where and how is it revealed?

....

....

✤ Darkness is our biggest takeaway from Job 3, but behind this darkness is hidden great hope. Job never actually experienced the dark he longed for, and he resents the light he still has. But his longing foreshadows another occasion of darkness, a time when someone experienced unrelenting anguish worse than Job's. Read Luke 23:44–46 and then note how the darkness in Job 3 foreshadows hope for God's people.

LET'S TALK

1. We've seen that the Lord puts "hedges" around his people, determining what's allowed to touch their lives. These divine hedges are meant to guard us in our relationship with the Lord and to deepen our dependence on him. As you consider the different "hedges" in Job's life (see 1:10; 3:23) as well as the ways in which God "hedges" all his people (look again at John 10:28–29; Romans 8:38–39; or Jude 24), where can you detect the Lord's "hedging" work in your own life?

2. We learn from Job that pouring out grief and despair is not a denial of our faith. It's simply being honest about our suffering and how very hard it is. Yet there are ways to lament that can dishonor the Lord and actually deepen our suffering. Do you think Job crossed that line? If so, how? Discuss ways in which lament can be both God-honoring and gut-level honest.

WHEN FRIENDSHIPS HURT

JOB 4:1-14:22

Years ago I lost a friend. No specific tragedy destroyed the relationship, nor did we casually drift apart. She chose to leave my life because I was a bad friend—an impatient friend. She'd been struggling at the time over a breakup with a man, and we'd spent hours together processing her pain, the disappointed hopes and feelings of rejection. But in time, I felt increasingly irritated. I couldn't understand why, with the passing of time and lots of support from friends, she couldn't seem to get over it. My impatience began to leak through in the short replies, changes of subject, and attempts to apply Bible verses like band-aids. It all came to a head one day when she shared how I was hurting her, and my own frustration poured out in rather harsh, critical words. That was it. Nothing I attempted to do or say afterward repaired the damage. It's not that all I said was wrong—it's that I tried to force her recovery to fit into my understanding of how it should go. We see that same sort of thing in this week's lesson in Job's back-and-forth dialogs with his three visiting friends. Job's friends—Eliphaz, Bildad, and Zophar—have listened to Job pour out his heart, and now they want a chance to weigh in. But what begins as a desire to help their suffering friend quickly turns argumentative, and they actually make things even harder for Job. Eliphaz, Bildad, and Zophar are confident that they know both the reason for Job's suffering and the remedy for it, but do they? We'll try to sort it out as we listen to this first of two rounds of speeches.

1. LEADER OF THE PACK (4:1–7:21)

The first of the friends to speak is Eliphaz, and he begins on a respectful note. There is wisdom in Eliphaz's approach: before leveling any criticism at Job, Eliphaz builds him up, enumerating all the good things Job has done to help people in times past. But after these few encouraging words, Eliphaz's tone quickly changes, and he accuses Job of being impatient and discouraged.

✦ Why, according to 4:6, does Eliphaz believe Job has every reason to hope that his suffering will end and his prosperity will resume?

....

....

....

....

The way Job's friends understand God—the framework that shapes how they view God and the world and people—is summarized in what Eliphaz says to Job in 4:7:

> "Remember: who that was innocent ever perished?
>   Or where were the upright cut off?"

✦ How would you explain this belief in your own words?

....

....

....

....

In 4:12–21 Eliphaz tells Job about a spiritual encounter he had.

✦ The spirit-voice makes suggestions to Eliphaz in 4:17, which he then shares with Job. How do these suggestions contradict the Lord's words in 1:8 and 2:3?

....

....

....

....

✤ As you consider how Eliphaz describes this encounter and what the spirit-voice says, who or what was the likely source of the experience?

> ### Eliphaz
>
> Eliphaz, from a region in Edom known for its wisdom, speaks first in all three cycles of speeches. He is the senior friend. We listen to what Eliphaz has to say while asking ourselves what he gets right and what he gets wrong.[10]

....

....

....

....

....

....

....

Some religions, like Hinduism and Buddhism, believe that our actions in this life project a force called *karma*, which determines the quality of our next life. Outside of those religions, there are just as many who believe that something like karma affects our day-to-day life—bad things happen to bad people and good things happen to good people. It's clear from Eliphaz's speech that he has a karma-like mindset. To Eliphaz's way of thinking, Job must have done something to bring all this trouble down on himself, even if what Job did wasn't bad enough to kill him.

✤ What in 5:17–18 does Eliphaz believe the Lord is doing in Job's life, and how does Eliphaz believe Job should respond in order for his prosperity to resume?

....

....

....

....

Eliphaz finishes his speech, and Job replies with an outpouring of emotion, first to the friends (6:1–7:10) and then directly to God (7:11–21).

*"In presenting us with so many speakers who
misunderstand their own situation and what God is doing,
the book of Job is nudging us to reflect on the limits of
our knowledge and on our ability to damage others
by assuming that we understand their situations."*[11]

✦ How does Job's response reveal how Eliphaz's speech has impacted him?

_____

_____

_____

_____

✦ What three things does Job say he will do in 7:11 as he redirects his response from the friends to the Lord himself?

1. _____

2. _____

3. _____

✦ How does Job view the Lord at this point in his suffering, and what specific things does he say in 7:11–21 that let you know?

_____

_____

_____

_____

Job asks:

> "What is man, that you make so much of him,
>   and that you set your heart on him,

> visit him every morning
>> and test him every moment?" (7:17–18)

✦ Some of the words Job pours out here are found also in Psalm 8:4–6, and these same words in the psalm are quoted much later in the New Testament to show their full meaning. Read the quote in Hebrews 2:5–9. What is revealed there that Job couldn't have seen way back in his day?

2. BOLD AND BLUNT (8:1–10:22)

Bildad jumps in next, and like Eliphaz before him, he thinks he has the answers Job needs.

✦ Unlike Eliphaz, who began his speech on a respectful note, Bildad is blunt and harsh from the outset. What does he say in 8:1–4 that could further discourage the hurting Job?

✦ What solution does Bildad propose for Job in 8:5–6?

Using images from nature—flowers and reeds and water and spiders' webs—Bildad makes his case that the righteous flourish while the wicked soon wither away to nothing. Then he cuts to the chase in 8:20, assuming that Job's withered condition is due to sin, that if Job will only acknowledge his guilt, his suffering will end.

Job agrees in theory with some of Bildad's argument (9:1–2), specifically that God is just and that God is also sovereign (fully in control) over absolutely everything that happens in this world. At the same time, Job knows he's done nothing to warrant such extreme suffering from God's hand. So he's utterly perplexed.

✦ What traits of God's character does Job illuminate in the following verses?

　　• 9:4

　　• 9:5–10

　　• 9:12

After responding to Bildad's speech, Job continues to pour out his heart, directing his words straight to the Lord in chapter 10.

✦ Review Job's lament in chapter 10, and then describe in a sentence or two how Job sees his relationship with the Lord at this point.

....

....

Because we have the entire Bible—Old and New Testaments—we can know more about God's ways and purposes than Job could know in his day. We have the whole story, while he had only a portion of it. Further, his intense suffering skewed the understanding of God that he did have. Pain can skew our understanding too sometimes, which is why it's so important to soak ourselves in God's word regularly.

✢ Psalm 103 is just one of countless Bible passages that shines the light of truth on skewed thinking about the Lord. In the chart that follows, jot down how Psalm 103 can serve as a corrective when, like Job, great suffering skews our own thinking.

Job 10	Psalm 103
vv. 1–2	vv. 1–2
vv. 3–7	vv. 3–5
vv. 8–9	vv. 6–8

Job 10	Psalm 103
vv. 14–17	vv. 9–12
vv. 18–19	vv. 13–14
vv. 20–22	vv. 15–19

3. HUFFING AND PUFFING (11:1–14:22)

Zophar doesn't even fake compassion when he addresses Job. He's outraged that Job doesn't share his convictions about God's ways, and he launches into a tirade against his suffering friend.

✦ What does Zophar say to Job in 11:1–6 that likely only increased Job's suffering?

Zophar goes on to describe—rightly—that God and his ways are beyond human understanding (11:7–12), and yet, at the same time, he presumes to understand God's reasons for Job's suffering!

✤ What does Zophar tell Job to do in 11:13–14, and what will it lead to (11:15–19)?

✤ How would you summarize Zophar's understanding of how God works in people's lives?

Job is getting fed up with his friends, and he begins his response to Zophar's speech in 12:1 by taking him down a notch, telling Zophar in so many words, "You think you've got all your theological *t*'s crossed and that you're wiser than everyone else."

✤ How does Job continue to push back against his friends in 12:3–4 and in 13:4–5?

As Job continues, he agrees in 12:7–12 with his friends that, yes, the Lord controls all things, including suffering. And then Job showcases God's majestic power—no one can tell God what to do (12:13–25). The Lord does whatever he pleases, reversing circumstances from good to bad and from bad to good.

✤ As Job speaks, the narrator records Job saying God's special name—Yahweh, or LORD, which our Bibles indicate with small capital letters—in 12:9. This is the only time Job uses this name, LORD, during these low points of his painful ordeal. The name indicates God's bond with his people, his covenant love. What does Job's use of God's special name during this painful time reveal about his heart for God?

....

....

....

....

✤ What desire does Job express in 13:3?

....

....

....

....

Job continues his pushback in 13:4–12 where he rebukes his friends, calling them "worthless physicians," and he says that they "whitewash with lies" (v. 4). He is trying to make his friends understand that they aren't helping him, not primarily because they're making him feel worse but because they're just plain wrong. They are trying to cover over—whitewash—what's happening to Job with their simplistic presumptions.

✤ After rebuking his friends, Job directs his words to the Lord himself, pouring his heart out in 13:20–28. What questions does Job ask God in this section, and what do those questions reveal about Job's deepest longing?

....

....

✣ Job gets real about death in chapter 14. Because of sin, everyone dies. No one escapes death. But in the middle of this, in verses 13–17, a bit of hope gets woven in. "Yes," he is saying, "death comes because of sin, but . . ." What hope underlies Job's gloomy realism?

LET'S TALK

1. Job's friends failed to comfort him. In fact, they made his suffering worse. Likely you can think of a time when the advice of a well-meaning friend caused more hurt than help when you were going through a crisis. How can you avoid making the same mistakes as Job's friends (and yours) when you are in a position to speak into the ordeal of a friend? Based on past experience, whether your own suffering or a friend's, touch on what helped and also what didn't.[12]

2. Job poured out his heart to God. His strong laments were filled with questions, and in his darkest hours, he said some things to God that we likely find quite shocking. Yet Job's laments, while painfully honest, were never irreverent. Discuss how studying Job's laments can change the way you relate to God when you don't understand what he's doing in your life.

....

....

....

....

....

....

....

DIGGING IN AND DOUBLING DOWN

JOB 15:1-21:34

The floppy ears of a basset hound drew my attention to the window. The dog, sitting directly in my line of vision, was resisting the repetitive tugs on its attached leash. The woman doing the tugging cajoled the hound to turn around and walk the way she wanted to go, but the dog wouldn't budge. Hidden behind the window shade, I watched the woman's frustration grow and the gentle tugs became longer and stronger, all to no avail. The dog stubbornly refused to turn and follow. The dog walker finally gave up and redirected her steps in the direction that the dog was determined to go. I was thankful that the window shade hid me from view because I was doubled over with laughter. On a much less humorous note, we see that same sort of stubbornness this week in Job's friends. Eliphaz, Bildad, and Zophar dig their heels in and insist that suffering is the direct and immediate result of sin. At the same time, Job insists that although he doesn't understand why he's suffering, he knows he's done nothing to bring it on himself. Adding to Job's pain is the callousness of his friends, a lack of compassion that springs from their heartless, clinical, wrong views of God. Eliphaz, Bildad, and Zophar are legalists with no real heart for God, and no heart for God inhibits a right understanding of God. So it's no wonder that in the midst of all this, Job is depressed, and he expects that he'll die quite soon. Even so, notes of hope come through once again during this second round of speeches.

1. ELIPHAZ DOUBLES DOWN (15:1–17:16)

We concluded last week with Job professing his innocence. He certainly hasn't claimed to be sinless, but he has insisted that there is no one-to-one correspondence between something he's done and his painful losses. Now the three friends, beginning here with Eliphaz, double down on their belief that suffering is the direct result of some particular sin.

✤ It's pretty clear from Eliphaz's opening words what he thinks of Job's viewpoint. How, in 15:1–14, does Eliphaz see Job's claims of blamelessness for his suffering?

In his speech (15:20–35), Eliphaz paints a picture of what happens to wicked people. And Eliphaz is right—evil doesn't prosper. But what Eliphaz gets very wrong here is *timing*. While evil doesn't prosper in the long run, it sometimes seems to pay off for a season. Eliphaz is right when he says that bad things happen to bad people—evil and evildoers will indeed be judged and destroyed. But he's wrong when he claims that tragedies and difficulties are the direct and immediate consequence of particular sins. The truth is, evil sometimes does seem to prosper—for a season. Sin *does* seem to pay off sometimes.

✤ While Eliphaz is right that evil is judged and punished, his understanding of how this plays out is way off base. What do we learn from the following passages about the ways of evil and how God deals with it?

· Psalm 73

· Matthew 13:24–30

✦ Eliphaz's callous heart is on full display in 15:31–35, where he makes cruel remarks about Job's children: "unripe grape," "blossom" (v. 33). What is Eliphaz implying about Job's kids in these verses?

✦ How, in 16:1–5, does Job assess his friends' approach to him in his pain?

✦ Job feels that the Lord is against him and treating him like an enemy, yet something different seems to lie underneath these hard feelings. What surprising note of confidence does Job express in 16:19?

✦ Job had been well regarded in his community, but his pathetic condition—not only his physical illness but his overwhelming grief—has changed how people view him. What particular changes are revealed in his lament in chapters 16–17?

✤ Job's illness is so bad that he believes he is about to die (17:1). If you recall, in Job's first lament (chapter 3), he wished for death as a way to escape the torment. Although he is still totally miserable and struggling with deep depression, how does 17:13–16 show us a subtle change in his thinking about his death?

....

....

....

....

✤ Despite the horror of his losses and the misery of his sickness, Job's greatest pain is feeling that the Lord has turned against him. It's not true, but at this point Job can't see it and suffers greatly in his bewilderment. In our day and age, because we have God's full revelation—the entire Bible—we have answers that Job did not, and we can identify hope hidden beneath his agonized words. We can see how Job's great suffering actually foreshadows the one whom God did turn away from—Jesus Christ. Job was blameless in causing his losses, but he wasn't sinless. Jesus, on the other hand, was both blameless and sinless. Look back over chapters 16 and 17 and note below where you can detect these gospel glimpses. To get some guidance, you might want to look first at Psalm 22:6–7; Isaiah 53:3; and Matthew 27:39–46.

....

....

....

....

....

> *Foreshadow: "to represent, indicate,*
> *or typify beforehand. To prefigure."*[13]

....

2. BILDAD DOUBLES DOWN (18:1-19:29)

Bildad launches into his second speech, and he's as indignant as Eliphaz was before him. Who is Job to refuse the counsel of his friends? Bildad can't stand it, so he sets out to paint a picture for Job, a stark picture of what happens to sinful people.

✦ How does Bildad use the following images in his description?

· Light and darkness

· Trap or snare

· Tent or dwelling place

✦ To what does Bildad attribute someone's suffering in 18:7–8?

The teaching of the Bible overall shows us that Bildad's portrait of an evil person is actually quite accurate. But his understanding of how it plays out is all wrong. First, we know that Job isn't suffering because he committed some sin, but Bildad won't believe that there isn't some direct connection. Second, Bildad doesn't get that justice—when awful things befall evil people—is often delayed and sometimes won't be evident until Jesus returns on judgment day.

✦ Job responds to Bildad with anguish in 19:1–3. What effect is his friends' counsel having on him?

....

....

....

....

✦ Job's three friends are proving to be no comfort whatsoever. Isn't it true that we sometimes don't know the depth or quality of a friendship until it's tested by a crisis of some sort? But these weren't the only relationships impacted by Job's suffering, which we see clearly in 19:13–19. Summarize in a sentence or two the extent of this impact.

....

....

....

....

✦ Job's words in 19:25–27 surprise us because they stand in sharp contrast to all his discouraged, beaten-down cries. We see here that underneath his perplexity about God, there are three things that Job knows—"For I know . . . ," he begins in verse 25. Identify these three things in 19:25–27.

1. ....

2. ....

3. ....

In the Bible, a redeemer, sometimes called a "kinsman-redeemer," was someone who took on the responsibility of providing for a family member. God is, of course, the supreme Redeemer of every member of his family, rescuing and providing for his people all through the Old Testament and then, ultimately, redeeming them from the terrible consequences of sin through the death of Jesus Christ on the cross. So even in the midst of his spiritual struggle, Job believes that God can and will redeem him—even if he dies—in such a way that all his doubts and questions about God will be joyfully answered.

3. ZOPHAR DOUBLES DOWN (20:1–21:34)

Zophar builds on what Bildad said in his last speech about the bad things that happen to bad people, but Zophar takes it one step further—his words paint more of an eternal picture. Not only does a sinner suffer immediate consequences, but those consequences go on and on and on. This is what hell will be like. He vividly describes the inescapable destiny of those who experience God's judgment.

✦ What aspects of Zophar's description of hell in chapter 20 strike you most forcefully?

....

....

....

....

✦ With what truth does Job contradict his friends in 21:7–13?

....

....

....

....

✦ Job exposes the heart of wicked people in 21:14–16. What characteristics of a wicked heart does he identify in these verses?

....

....

✦ What point does Job make in 21:22–26? How is this reinforced in Ecclesiastes 9:1–2?

> *"Job in his innocent suffering foreshadows the Lord Jesus Christ and his substitutionary and redemptive sufferings. Zophar's description helps us grasp more deeply what Jesus did for us. And . . . it helps shape our expectations of what the Christian life will be like this side of the resurrection. 'Through many tribulations we must enter the kingdom of God' (Acts 14:22)."[14]*

LET'S TALK

1. We can't help but notice in this second round of speeches that all three of Job's friends have become agitated. They are indignant that Job won't embrace their belief that he's suffering because he sinned in some way. Eliphaz, Bildad, and Zophar are upset because, if Job is right that his suffering isn't because he sinned, then *they* might be liable to suffering too. By holding tightly to their viewpoint, they can avoid ending up like Job. In what areas of life might we be tempted to cling to a particular interpretation of God's word and ways even when we're shown sound evidence to the contrary? Some of us might be a bit scared to face what God's word says about divine election, for example. Others of us might want to avoid considering the Bible's teaching

on a wife's submission to her husband. Talk about specific areas where avoidance might be a temptation personally, and then identify some truths about God that can take away those temptations and the fears that underlie them.

2. If only Job could know at this point what we know about his situation. And we want to tell him, don't we? We want so badly to be able to step in and alleviate his suffering and fan into flame those glimmers of hope that spark up in this week's lesson. How much more do we want to alleviate the suffering of someone we know and love personally! We've already been warned how not to be like Job's friends—what not to say and do—and sometimes just listening is the best thing. But there is a time to speak up as well. When we do, we want to share words that fuel hope. Select at least one of the following passages and discuss how it equips you with hope and prepares you to speak with care to a suffering friend: Psalms 42–43; Lamentations 3:22–25; Romans 5:1–5; 1 Peter 1:3–8.

GOLD IN THE DUST

JOB 22:1-27:23

Is it ever going to end? We can't help but wonder as we come to yet another round of speeches, the verbal combat between Job and his three friends Eliphaz, Bildad, and Zophar. If you are feeling a bit weary, not only of Job's misery but of the repetitive arguments, just imagine how weary Job was at this point! This is the third and final round of speeches between Job and the friends, but this round has some definite differences. For one thing, the friends have less to say. In fact, only Eliphaz gives a full-on speech this time. Bildad utters just a few words, and Zophar says nothing at all. It's as though they've run out of steam. They've said all they can say. Job, however, is far from done. He might be sick and tired of arguing with his friends, but he's driven to press on because he's desperate to find God in his pain. He wants to understand not only *where* God is in his situation, but *who* God is in it. "Oh, that I knew where I might find him, that I might come even to his seat!" Job cries (23:3). That's the compelling passion that sustains Job during these dark days.

1. PEOPLE WHO LIVE IN GLASS HOUSES . . . (22:1-30)

Eliphaz begins his third speech by trying one final time to prove that his view of God is right and Job's is wrong. He begins by asking, "Can a man be profitable to God?" Eliphaz's point is that human beings can do nothing to obligate God to bless them. Technically speaking, he's right, of course, but because Eliphaz has no concept of God as relational, his underlying theology is seriously messed up here. Eliphaz believes that God stays distant from people and just lets the chips fall where they may. Good people get blessed and bad people suffer. Period. He simply doesn't understand a loving, caring God who works out his purposes in someone's life—work that includes both pain and pleasure, gain and loss.

✦ Eliphaz accuses Job of all kinds of sins in 22:5–9. How does Job 1:1 show us how we are to think about Eliphaz's accusations?

....

....

....

....

Eliphaz counsels Job in 22:21 to "agree" with God so that his circumstances will improve. In other words, Eliphaz assumes that his view of Job's suffering—that it's due to sin—is also God's view, and if Job will just get on board, his misery will soon end. Eliphaz illustrates how someone can have strong theological convictions and an advanced theological vocabulary but still be theologically way off the rails.

Eliphaz sets up conditions for Job's recovery in 22:23–25: If Job does certain righteous deeds, then good things will come his way. We can't help but see echoes of Satan's accusation at the beginning of the book, when he accused Job of worshiping God only because God prospered his life. So here, if Job were to take Eliphaz's advice, he'd be doing exactly what Satan had accused him of earlier—bartering for blessing. So far Job hasn't caved to the pressure. And his refusal to cave proves that integrity and his relationship with God matter more to him than renewed health or prosperity.

✦ As Job's friend, Eliphaz no doubt knew that Job had been a wealthy man. So one of the conditions Eliphaz sets before Job concerns gold, the finest gold in the known world at that time, the gold of Ophir. Much of Job's wealth was likely lost when his farm was wiped out, yet Eliphaz speaks here as though Job still has much gold to contend with. If Job gives up this gold, how, according to Eliphaz in 22:25–27, will it impact Job's relationship with God?

....

....

✦ How does Jesus's encounter with the rich young ruler in Matthew 19:16–24 shed light on the truth of Eliphaz's instructions to Job here?

Eliphaz is correct in principle. When earthly things—possessions, relationships, or personal achievements—mean too much to us, God means too little, and he gets displaced from the throne of our heart. So in this Eliphaz is right. He's dead wrong, however—yet again—in his application. Job has never valued his wealth and success more than God.

2. A DISCOURAGED SOUL (23:1–24:25)

Job's weariness is evident in his reply to Eliphaz, and as we read it, we can't help but notice that he devotes his attention more to the Lord than to arguing further with his friends.

✦ What desire does Job express in 23:1–3?

✦ What fantasy does Job describe in 23:4–7, and how does the fantasy end?

✦ We're back to reality in 23:8–9, where Job can't seem to find God or get a handle on what God is doing. Despite the fact that God seems distant, what confidence does Job express in 23:10?

God's absolute control of everything gives Job hope, but at the same time, it makes him afraid (23:13–15). His fear certainly doesn't spring from a guilty conscience, as we know, and Job has just declared again, in verses 11–12, that he's done nothing to cause his suffering. So why does God's governing of his circumstances terrify him? Most likely it's that his awareness of God's control simply exposes how little control Job actually has. And that can be scary when life isn't going well, right? We welcome and rejoice in the sovereignty of God when it seems to be safeguarding us in happy circumstances. But when that same sovereignty lets our life fall apart, we realize that our loving God lets in the bad as well as the good. And that's frightening.

Still thinking about God's overarching control of the whole world, Job questions in chapter 24 why, given such control, God doesn't intervene faster and more visibly to right wrongs and fix what's broken in the world.

✦ What about God's ways baffles Job in 24:2–12?

✤ In 24:13 Job mentions "those who rebel against the light, who are not acquainted with its ways, and do not stay in its paths." How does the rest of chapter 24 clarify what he means?

....

....

....

....

....

....

....

....

....

Sovereignty
"God is King and Lord of all. . . ." He is sovereign over everything, which means that "nothing happens without God's willing it to happen, willing it to happen before it happens, and willing it to happen in the way that it happens."[15] God governs everything that happens in this world and in each individual life.

3. BILDAD'S BLINDNESS (25:1–6)

Bildad has run out of steam, it seems, because his final words to Job are wrapped up in six short verses. Bildad does agree with Job about at least one aspect of God's character—God's sovereignty. And Bildad seems to know that nothing in creation can match the purity and power of God. But Bildad is still way off base. He's trying to make the point that "Job's desire and hope to stand before God face-to-face is absurd and arrogant."[16]

✤ How does Genesis 1:26–31 show that Bildad's assessment of human beings in 25:6 is flat-out wrong?

....

....

....

....

> *"The friends have argued their theological understanding and . . . they have consistently thought of the choice before them as being that either God or Job must be in the wrong. On account of Job's suffering and their own confidence about being able to interpret it, the friends have never really brought their own viewpoint under scrutiny or given thought to the possibility that they may be wrong in both their defense of God and their pursuit of Job."*[17]

4. THE HAND OF GOD (26:1–27:23)

Now Job gives his final response to these three friends. Their time together has been exhausting and hasn't helped Job one iota. That being said, we have noticed a subtle change in Job during all the back and forth with Eliphaz, Bildad, and Zophar. As Job has defended himself and his righteousness before God, his convictions have actually deepened in the process, and along with that, we've seen more glimmers of hope. Like exercise strengthens muscles, vigorous debate can strengthen hearts when it is undergirded by faith.

Sarcasm drips from Job's tongue as he lets his friends know how totally unhelpful they have been (26:1–4). "It is almost as if Job posts on social media: 'Just been listening to eight wonderful speeches from the wisest men on earth. I have been having some difficulties and sadness recently, and they've really helped me so much. Not!'"[18]

In 26:5–13, Job recounts God's magnificent work in creation—the world and every realm above and below the earth—and he finishes his beautiful words with this:

> "Behold, these are but the outskirts of his ways,
>   and how small a whisper do we hear of him!
>   But the thunder of his power who can understand?" (26:14)

✢ What point is he making to his friends?

"And Job again took up his discourse, and said . . ." That's how the narrator begins chapter 27, and these opening words indicate that Job is about to say something really important.

✧ What specific commitments does Job make in 27:4–6?

✧ In 27:7–12, Job speaks to his friends as though they are his enemies. What warning does he give to them in these verses?

✧ Job goes on to describe in 27:13–23 what will happen to people who harm the faith of God's children or cause them to suffer for their faith. We find here a very strong warning of how God's judgment will play out for those who aren't saved in Christ Jesus. Note below the ways in which God's judgment will impact the guilty:

· Family:

· Home and material possessions:

....

....

....

· Heart and mind:

....

....

....

LET'S TALK

1. God's sovereignty has been on full display this week. This attribute of God—his sovereignty—is meant to be a source of comfort rather than anxiety or fear. How does having a deeper grasp of God's sovereignty shape your perspective on your current circumstances and how you might respond to them? Consider how a deeper awareness of God's sovereignty can serve as a guide not only for how to think about your life but also for how to pray in various situations.

....

....

....

....

....

....

....

2. Job has withstood his friends' accusations, that he brought his suffering on himself through sin. What strengthens him to hold fast his conviction is a clear conscience: "My heart does not reproach me for any of my days," he declares in 27:6. Our conscience is a gift from God, a built-in awareness of right and wrong. We are responsible to let our conscience be shaped by the standards of God's word, by how the Bible defines right and wrong, and we must be careful not to ignore our conscience when it nudges us. Job's conscience helped him withstand his friends' bad counsel. Discuss how your conscience has guided your walk with the Lord. Can you think of a time when your conscience has fostered growth in godliness? Conversely, have you ever violated your conscience, trying to suppress its nudges? If so, what was the result?[19]

TREASURE HUNT

JOB 28:1-28

Job has suffered enormous losses—his livelihood, his children, his health—yet what seems to haunt him most of all is how these losses have caused him to question everything he thought he knew about God. How could God have let his life fall apart so drastically? What provoked God's wrath against him? His friends insist that Job must have committed some significant sin, but he's confident that he didn't. And all their back-and-forth debating hasn't solved this mystery. So where can Job find answers? Where is wisdom to be found? That's what he's desperate to find out.

Here in chapter 28, we find a poem about wisdom. We are devoting a whole week to this poem because it seems to stand alone in the book, to stand apart from the material that comes in the chapters immediately before and after the poem. Because it stands alone, some Bible scholars think that someone besides Job is reciting the poem, but it's just as likely that Job himself is the one reciting it since it's placed in the middle of his final speech. Ultimately, it's okay to be unsure. What matters most for Bible study is the poem itself, not who actually penned it. Even so, here in our study, we're going to assume that it was written by Job.

1. HIDDEN TREASURE (28:1-11)

Job paints an enchanting picture of wisdom as precious treasure buried deep in a cavernous mine. This beautiful wisdom is hidden, and it is very difficult to find. In fact, it's almost inaccessible. Even so, the poem hints that it's available to those who are willing to make the effort to find it. All this mirrors Job's dilemma, doesn't it? He has been desperate to understand why God has let him suffer so much and why God seems so far away from Job in his pain. No answers have come, yet from time to time Job has given us glimpses of hope. He is still searching for hidden treasure.

✦ What words does Job use in verses 1–6 to showcase the beauty of wisdom?

....

....

....

....

✦ In verses 7–11, Job clarifies that only human beings, not animals, have any hope of uncovering wisdom from the deep and bringing it out of darkness into the light. What, according to this passage, is involved in pursuing it?

....

....

....

....

....

"The fear of the Lord, awe and reverence before God, is the beginning of wisdom. And when we are befuddled and confused by things that we cannot understand in this world, we look not for specific answers always to specific questions, but we look to know God in His holiness, in His righteousness, in His justice, and in His mercy. Therein is the wisdom that is found in the book of Job."[20]

✦ The book of Proverbs is all about wisdom—what it is and how to get it. The beautiful poetry here in Job 28 shows us wisdom hidden in a mine, but Proverbs gives us practical ways to dig down into the mine to uncover it. Note how the proverbs in the chart below help us uncover the riches of wisdom.

Mining the Riches of Wisdom		
	How to Mine	*What Is Found*
Proverbs 2:1–5		
Proverbs 8:17		
Proverbs 13:10		
Proverbs 17:24		
Proverbs 19:20		

✦ How do the following passages reveal more of the hidden riches in Job's poem?

· Psalm 119:18–19

....

....

....

....

....

....

· Isaiah 33:5–6

....

....

....

....

....

....

· Matthew 13:44–46

....

....

....

The Wisdom Books of the Bible

Biblical wisdom can be defined as "skill in the art of godly living, or more fully, that orientation which allows one to live in harmonious accord with God's ordering of the world."[21] Most of the Bible's "Wisdom Books" contain a good bit of poetry. The Bible books that fall into this category are Job, Proverbs, Ecclesiastes, and Song of Solomon. Psalms is often included in the category too, because the Psalter contains "wisdom psalms" and lots of poetry.

---

2. BUT WHERE? (28:12–19)

Job shows even more clearly the impossibility of uncovering God's wisdom. He begins the section with a question: "But where shall wisdom be found?" (v. 12). This one short question basically sums up the theme of the entire book. Job's yearning to know—to find answers to his questions about God and suffering—has been the driving force of all he's said so far.

✦ What comparisons to wisdom are set out in verses 12–19?

✦ What is this passage, verses 12–19, designed to teach us?

3. AN ANSWER—AT LAST (28:20-28)

Job repeats his question from 28:12 at the beginning of this section: "From where, then, does wisdom come?" (v. 20).

✦ In the first part of the poem, in 28:1–11, Job hinted at the possibility that people can seek and perhaps even uncover the glories of wisdom. How do his words in verses 21–22 paint a different picture?

✦ How does Job's question begin to be answered in verse 23?

✿ To what work of God does Job link wisdom in verses 24–27? Take a look also at Proverbs 8:22–31.

....

....

....

....

Job has so desperately sought to understand what underlies his suffering, even more so after his friends have insisted that it's due to sin. We know that Job has held his ground against his friends' accusations, but all the debating has surely provoked his questions. "Okay, God," he likely thought, "I know I did nothing to bring this on myself, so what *is* the reason?" Now, for the first time since the beginning of the book, God speaks in verse 28. Job has asked where wisdom can be found, but rather than answer directly, God reframes the question. Instead of telling Job *where* wisdom is, he tells him *what* it is—the fear of the Lord.

✿ What do we learn from the following passages about what it means to fear the Lord?

· Psalm 34:11–14

....

....

....

· Luke 12:4–7

....

....

....

✿ Compare God's words in 28:28—"the fear of the Lord, that is wisdom"—to the very first verse of the book (1:1). Considered together, how do these two verses affirm that the three friends are completely wrong about the reason for Job's suffering?

✤ Job doesn't see it yet, but this beautiful poem hides within it the seeds of the answer to his deepest question: "Where shall wisdom be found?" (v. 12). What do the following passages reveal about the answer?

· 1 Corinthians 1:22–24

· Colossians 2:1–3

> "'Behold, the fear of the Lord, that is wisdom, and to turn away from evil is understanding' (Job 28:28). How we respond to this verse is a litmus test for our hearts. In a saying that is crucial to the whole book, God directs our attention away from our agonized questions and toward himself. He does not take us by the hand and lead us to the answers; rather, he beckons us to bow before the Lord himself."[22]

LET'S TALK

1. In the Job 28 poem, searching for wisdom is like mining for hidden treasure. How do *we* do that, practically speaking? Talk about what we can expect to find as we search.

....

....

....

....

....

....

2. Our response to difficulty reveals our hearts. When trouble comes, or even when you simply can't understand why your life isn't working out the way you'd hoped, what's your default reaction? Our main take-away this week is that what we need most isn't an explanation or even a change of circumstances. What does this poem in Job 28 reveal as our greatest need?

....

....

....

....

....

....

....

WEEK 7

THE GOOD OLD DAYS

JOB 29:1-31:40

Looking back—it's something we're all tempted to do from time to time. We look back to something we once had—health, wealth, success, a relationship—that's now lost to us, perhaps forever. When life in the past seems so much better than life in the present, we're tempted to fix our gaze backward, to that earlier time that was so much happier than today. Focusing on the past is dangerous, as the preacher in Ecclesiastes points out: "Say not, 'Why were the former days better than these?' For it is not from wisdom that you ask this" (Ecclesiastes 7:10). But that's exactly where we find Job this week, caught up in nostalgia as he looks back on what his life was like before tragedy struck. His backward focus, these memories of the good old days, just makes his present look all the more bleak, and it compels him to pour out his heart to God one final time.

1. A BACKWARD LOOK (29:1-25)

Chapter 29 begins a new section, which we know from the way it begins: "And Job again took up his discourse . . ." (29:1). We saw that same wording at the beginning of chapter 27. It's how the narrator moves the story forward.

✦ Job looks back on his life and recounts what he used to have. What losses does he name in verses 2–6?

_____

_____

✦ Of the losses Job names in verses 2–6, which one seems to grieve him most?

Job recalls his former reputation, the respect he was shown by young and old alike. The city gate was the heartbeat of the community. Business deals were transacted there, and justice was handed down in civil matters. The most prominent citizens, like Job, had "a seat in the square."

✦ List the reasons Job gives in 29:12–17 for his stellar reputation.

In those good old days, Job's future seemed bright, and he imagined that his position was secure (29:18–20).

✦ Back in those days, why, according to verses 21–25, did people seek out Job?

2. BUT NOW . . . (30:1–31)

Job's good old days are long past, and his high standing in the community has shattered.

✢ What sort of people are Job's tormentors in 30:1–10, and what does their mockery indicate about the extent of Job's fall from favor?

....

....

....

....

✢ What reason does Job give in 30:11 for why these tormentors believe they can get away with mistreating him?

....

....

....

....

✢ As Job recounts the abuse he's experiencing, his grief overwhelms him, coloring once again his understanding of God. What are the ways in which Job sees God acting toward him in 30:19–23?

....

....

....

....

Job's words express hopelessness, but they also reveal a hidden hope. After all, it is *God* to whom Job turns, and he does so with raw honesty. So despite his spiritual depression, he still believes. And this man, Job, one who "fears the Lord" (we defined this fear of the Lord last week, so take a look back at that lesson if you need a refresher), is also very real with God as he expresses his thoughts and feelings.

✦ What do the images of light and dark and the color black convey in 30:24–31?

....

....

....

....

3. ONE MORE TIME (31:1-40)

Job makes a final plea to God in chapter 31, arguing his case once more that he has done nothing to cause his misery. After all, he writes, God knows everything about him (v. 4), so God would know if Job had been living in sin. First, Job is innocent of sexual sin. Job declares the commitment—the covenant—he had made to stop sexual lust before it could lodge in his mind (v. 1). From there he catalogs other areas of life in which he's been faithful and righteous.

✦ In 31:5–8, Job reinforces the fact that he has lived as a wise man. The language in these verses, particular words and phrases, is found all through the Bible's Wisdom Literature, which, if you recall, includes not only Job but also Proverbs, Ecclesiastes, Song of Solomon, and some of the psalms. Read Psalm 1, a wisdom psalm, and note one or two similarities to what Job describes here in 31:5–8.

....

....

....

....

Job returns to sexual purity in 31:9–12. Here it's not so much about lust as about faithfulness in marriage. Job has not committed adultery. If he had, he says, the law of retribution should be enacted—another man coming along and taking *his* wife. But Job wouldn't call this down on himself if he had some secret immorality or picadillo hiding in his past. He knows he's been faithful both to his own marriage and the marriages of others.

✦ How, according to 31:13–23, has Job acted blamelessly toward others?

....

....

✦ Job declares himself innocent of idolatry in 31:24–28. During his prosperous years, what idols does Job say he resisted?

· 31:24–25

· 31:26–27

✦ How would worshiping these things, thereby making them into idols, have impacted Job's walk with God? (See 31:28)

✦ How, according to the following verses, has Job lived righteously?

· 31:29–30

· 31:31–32

· 31:33–34

After declaring his innocence, Job pleads with God to answer him. If he is blameless—and he is—then why is God treating him so cruelly? Job has had moments during his ordeal when an accurate view of God broke through his spiritual fog, but for the most part, he's seen God as callous and unkind. And if he is actually wrong—if Job has done something bad that he simply cannot see—then he is desperate to know what it is. Why won't God answer? That's where Job leaves it—"the words of Job are ended" (31:40).

✦ This is the last time Job will plead his innocence. He has never wavered in his conviction that he did nothing to bring such suffering into his life. As we listen to Job, we likely think, *I'd never dare declare myself innocent! I know how much I sin!* So we can't help but wonder whether Job is trying to sidestep the sin issue. Sure, he's lived a righteous life, but to get out from under great suffering by appealing to his good works, well, it seems a bit arrogant to our ears, a bit self-righteous. And it would be, were it not for the fact that all his declarations of innocence actually point to something else—the innocence of someone else. What does Romans 3:21–24 reveal about why Job's declarations are acceptable and wonderfully true?

"Job's prayers will be answered, but only when his sufferings have achieved that for which God purposed them. In a deeper way it was the same for Jesus Christ. In a similar way it is yet the same for Christian people today; when God remains silent in answer to our urgent cries, it is not that he does not hear, but rather that it is somehow necessary for us to cry in vain and wait in hope until he achieves in us, and in his world, what he wills to achieve."[23]

LET'S TALK

1. We see from Job, and from Ecclesiastes 7:10, that looking back on happier times can be dangerous. Nostalgia is more than fond memories—so often it's memories with the reality stripped out. When the present is difficult, it's easy to sugarcoat the past; we forget that there was a reason why that earlier chapter in our lives ended. In what sort of circumstances can a backward look actually prove helpful? Discuss some possibilities. Talk also about the opposite—times when looking back is likely to be harmful.

2. Job concludes his final speech by declaring his faithfulness to God's ways. He's not trying to bargain with God for blessing; he's just declaring once again that his conscience is clear. Through a set of conditional statements—"*If* I have done such and such, *then* let me experience such and such a consequence"—he shows how he's sought to live by God's ways in every area of life. Only someone with a clear conscience would dare pray this way! What specific things on Job's "integrity list" either convict or inspire you in your walk with God?

_____

_____

_____

_____

_____

_____

_____

WOUNDS OF A FAITHFUL FRIEND

JOB 32:1-37:24

Arguing is exhausting. The mental and emotional drain of making our case and defending it leaves us wrung out. But it can be almost just as tiring listening to the arguments of others, whether it's bickering children in the back seat or adults on Twitter. No doubt we're definitely feeling that weariness at this point in our Job study. The debate between Job and his three friends—Eliphaz, Bildad, and Zophar—has gone on and on and on. The friends believe that suffering is linked to sin, so since Job has been suffering terribly, there's no doubt in their minds that he's committed terrible sin. But Job has stood his ground in this three-against-one verbal battle, refusing to bend. He's convinced that his sin is not the cause of his incredible losses. Last week we reached a milestone—Job's friends finally quit trying to convince him, and Job had the last word. Even so, Job still doesn't have an answer to the deepest cry of his soul: "Why, God, why?" So there's a bit of a recap about where we've come so far.

Now, this week, we meet someone new, a friend named Elihu, and he's more than ready to have a turn to speak. He's stayed quietly behind the scenes listening, but he just can't keep quiet any longer. And once he begins talking, he continues with no interruptions for six entire chapters! As Elihu talks, some light begins to dawn, light that will grow even brighter later and finally dispel Job's darkness.

1. VOICE OF WISDOM (32:1–33:33)

Elihu appears for the first time in chapter 32, but he's been here in the story, behind the scenes, all along. Although he is late to appear, his role is not insignificant. One way we know he's not just a bit player is that the narrator includes Elihu's background—he's from the Ram family, the son of Barachel the Buzite (32:2). Narrators often don't bother to include the personal information of minor characters. We learn also that Elihu is a young man. We aren't given his actual age, but all we need to know is that he was young compared to the ages of Job and the other three friends.

✦ Four times in the first five verses of chapter 32, we're told that Elihu "burned with anger." What reasons are given for his anger?

· Elihu's anger at Job:

....

....

....

· Elihu's anger at the three friends:

....

....

....

✦ What do we learn in 32:6–10 about why Elihu is just now speaking out?

....

....

....

....

✦ Given his young age, why, according to 32:8, does Elihu feel confident to speak?

....

....

Elihu had listened to the three friends' speeches, waiting to hear them counsel Job with wisdom, but they'd failed. And finally they gave up altogether on Job, clinging to their own idea of wisdom. So Elihu boldly rebukes them, and then, in chapter 33, he addresses Job directly. Unlike the three know-it-all friends, Elihu has a much more humble approach to Job, telling him, "I am toward God as you are; I too was pinched off from a piece of clay" (33:6). And then Elihu recounts what Job has been saying about God, that even though Job is blameless, God treats him like an enemy and refuses to answer him. In this, Job is all wrong, Elihu tells him (33:8–13).

✦ God does speak, Elihu declares in 33:14, even when people aren't consciously aware of it. What in 33:16–18 does God communicate at such times?

....

....

....

....

✦ Elihu points out another way God "speaks" in 33:19–28. What is that way, and what is God's purpose in it?

....

....

....

....

God intends in his speaking, whether in someone's conscience (33:16–18) or in painful circumstances (33:19–28), to bring about deliverance, and the words Elihu uses to describe this redemptive work of God point centuries into the future to God's ultimate deliverance for sinners and sufferers, the only mediator between God and man, Jesus Christ. Elihu speaks of a "mediator," one who will deliver the sufferer "from going down into the pit" (33:23–24), and when that mediator comes, the sufferer cries out, "I have found a ransom" (33:24). He then turns fully to the Lord in faith, repentance, and joy (33:25–27), and he is able to see that this mediator has redeemed him from death and brought him out into the light (33:28).

All through our study, Job has longed to hear from God and to be delivered from his painful ordeal, but what he—and we—need most is the deliverance that comes only through Jesus. Even though, as in Job's case, there is often no direct connection between our suffering and particular sins we commit, sin is still the underlying cause of all misery in this world. Suffering is a foretaste of a holy God's judgment, which sinners deserve to experience, and because we are all sinners, we all deserve to suffer. That's why our greatest need isn't rescue from painful circumstances; it's rescue from sin. And God has provided it! He sent a mediator, one who ransomed us from the suffering we deserve by taking it on himself instead. So right here, coming from the mouth of the young man Elihu, are glimmers of eternal hope and the best news ever.

✦ Not only does God speak to people in their conscience and through their circumstances; he does so not grudgingly but abundantly (33:29). What, according to 33:30, is God's ultimate purpose in the varied ways he speaks?

....

....

....

....

2. GOD IS GOD! (34:1–35:16)

Elihu launches straight away into this second speech in chapter 34, which is followed immediately by his third speech in chapter 35. We know where to mark off each of his speeches because each one begins with words like, "Then Elihu answered and said . . ." (32:6; 34:1; 35:1; and 36:1).

Elihu begins his second speech by addressing "wise men" (34:2). Most likely, he has an audience that includes not only Job and the other three friends but also the old sages of the community. Despite this daunting audience, Elihu has no qualms about voicing strong criticism of Job, pointing out how Job's faulty view of God (that God is unfair) places Job on par with evildoers (34:5–9). And then Elihu points out precisely why Job's view of God is so very wrong.

> *"The suffering of the righteous is not a token of God's enmity but of his love. It is not a punishment of their sins but a refinement of their righteousness. It is not a preparation for destruction, but a protection from destruction."*[24]

✤ What does Elihu declare about God in 34:10–15?

· 34:10

· 34:11

· 34:12

· 34:13–15

Elihu sees God's justice in terms of *fairness*. God could never be unfair—it would go against his very character. His point is, when Job accuses God of being unjust, he's speaking folly about the one who controls the life and death of every living thing.

✦ Elihu turns to Job in 34:16 and begins to speak directly to him, detailing more of God's sovereign power and justice, and in light of those divine attributes, Elihu penetrates to the core of Job's faulty perspective about God: "When he is quiet, who can condemn? When he hides his face, who can behold him, whether it be a nation or a man?" (34:29). Elihu makes a profound point here, which is that while Job isn't suffering because he sinned, he *is* sinning in his suffering. What sin of Job's is exposed by Elihu's questions in 34:29?

✦ How in 34:37 does Elihu summarize Job's accusations against God?

✦ In Elihu's third speech (chapter 35), he shows how Job's thinking about God has changed—and the change isn't positive. Somewhere along the way, Job began to question the benefit of living a righteous life: "What advantage have I? How am

I better off than if I had sinned?" (35:3). What does this question reveal about how Job has come to view his relationship with God?

Elihu rebukes Job's question with a big dose of reality in 35:5–8, pointing out that God isn't swayed by what human beings do or don't do, whether good or evil. In fact, Elihu says, multitudes of people cry out for help, but God doesn't answer (35:9–13).

✦ What reason does Elihu give in verses 12–13 for why God disregards some cries for help?

3. THE POWER OF GOD (36–37)

Elihu delivers his fourth and final speech in chapters 36 and 37, and here he makes the case that God, and God alone, is qualified to determine what is just and what isn't. Elihu's final speech is good preparation for what will come afterward—hearing directly from God himself (we'll get to this in Week 9). Like the Old Testament prophets, Elihu claims to speak for God in what he's about to say (36:2–4).

✦ What does Elihu say about God in 36:5?

> *"The lesson Elihu teaches us here is that it is not age that brings wisdom but the Spirit of God. There is no necessary correlation between grey hair and good theology. There is no necessary connection between a wizened face and a wise heart."*[25]

✛ How, in verses 36:6–10, is God's justice worked out?

....

....

....

✛ When people experience suffering, as Elihu says, God uses the experience to draw the sufferers to himself. What two possible responses to God does Elihu identify in 36:11–12?

....

....

....

....

✛ In 36:13 we get a glimpse inside the heart of those who reject God. What do we see there?

....

....

....

....

✦ What is revealed in 36:15 about God's purposes in people's suffering?

....

....

....

....

✦ What warning does Elihu give Job in 36:21?

....

....

....

....

✦ The final verses of chapter 36 and most of chapter 37 are utterly God-focused. What does Elihu reveal about God in each of the following passages?

· 36:26–31

....

....

....

· 37:10–13

....

....

....

✦ According to 37:14–24, what is Elihu's purpose in painting this majestic word-portrait of God?

....

....

....

....

LET'S TALK

1. Elihu is angry at his elders—at Eliphaz, Bildad, Zophar, and at Job—because they have dishonored God in their words and thoughts. Last week Job listed all the specific ways he'd lived a righteous life, but Elihu's anger exposes what grieves God most of all—believing bad things about God and thereby dishonoring him. Discuss how Elihu portrays God in his speeches. How can his portrayal of God reshape our own view, even when—maybe especially when—we are suffering?

....

....

....

....

....

....

....

2. What is your deepest longing in times of suffering? Of course you want relief! The desire for pain to end is part of what it means to be human. That's why it's so surprising that Job never once asks for his losses to be restored. His longing is totally vertical—for God himself. How has God used your own seasons of difficulty to intensify your longing for him?

If you are struggling with difficulty in the present, how is the struggle impacting your longing for God, and what are you doing about it?

_____

_____

_____

_____

_____

_____

_____

THE ANSWER TO EVERYTHING

JOB 38:1–41:34

God rarely comes in ways we've been expecting. Have you noticed? Answers to prayer are so often different—and amazingly superior—to what we had in mind. Even when God says no to our requests, his *no* carries with it the seeds to an even better yes. That's exactly what happens to Job. Throughout his long ordeal, he's wanted to hear from God, and now he finally does. At the same time, what he hears is not at all what he was expecting. It's actually so much more that it stuns him into silence and radically changes his heart. That's how God works. Job has wanted to know the reason for his suffering. Instead of answering *why*, God answers *who*—who made the world and controls the world and therefore governs every aspect of the world? And shockingly God's control extends even to the evil things that happen. The Lord reveals to Job—and to us—that evil is not some independent superpower at war with God. From the beginning of time, evil has always been under God's control. So that leaves us asking, Is God the author of evil? We know from his character that he cannot be, but he reveals here that evil has a place in how God has hardwired the world to work—a place determined by God to ultimately work everything together for good for those who love him (Romans 8:28).

1. OUT OF THE WHIRLWIND (38:1–40:5)

Finally! What Job has longed for happens at last—he hears from God. We aren't told how exactly God communicates with Job, but we are given clues about the nature of God's approach. First and foremost, he comes to Job as "the Lord" (38:1). If you recall, whenever we see "Lord" with small capital letters, it signifies God's covenant name, Yahweh, and this name is meant to show God's relational heart toward his people. The only other time this name appears in the story is back in the beginning, in the heavenly council. Another clue about God's character, and in particular his heart for Job, is that he comes "out of the whirlwind" (38:1), by which is meant a big storm. This is not the only time in the Bible when God reveals himself in and through tumultuous weather, and each time it happens, he is revealing something about himself to his people. (If you have a few extra minutes this week, check out one or two of these other occurrences: Exodus 19; Psalm 18; and Matthew 14:22–33.)

"Lord" in Job

"The book records the character and dealings of the God of Israel with a believer before and outside of Israel. In this way, the drama of Job, although historically not set in Israel's story, is tied to the great story of the whole Bible with its fulfillment in Jesus Christ."[26]

It's amazing how often in the Bible we see the Lord asking people questions! He spoke to the prophets that way (1 Kings 19:9; Jonah 4:4). Later, Jesus asked lots of questions. If you take time to study the Gospels, you'll see that Jesus asked questions as a way to expose people's hearts (see, for example, Luke 14:1–6; John 5:2–9). And that's exactly how the Lord approaches Job. He asks Job question after question after question—not because the Lord needs answers but because Job does. Yet the answers Job is going to get are very different from the ones he thinks he needs.

✦ The Lord wants Job to think back to the beginning, to the time of creation and then to how the whole of creation functions. As you review 38:4–38, what big-picture takeaway do you think the Lord is conveying to Job—and to us—in his beautiful description?

✦ We associate the sea with fun and family vacations, but in ancient times, the sea was scary—necessary for travel and commerce, but filled with numerous dangers, such as the frequent and sudden storms that could arise and capsize boats. With that ancient perspective in mind, what do you think the Lord is communicating to Job in 38:8–11?

✦ Take a closer look at 38:39–41, where the Lord gets Job to think about two predatory animals—lions and ravens. The survival of these animals means that other creatures have to die.[27] The question God asks here is, Who feeds these predators? As we think about the answer to that question, what reality about God must we contend with?

✦ The Lord created each and every animal with a unique design, a number of which are described for Job—and us—in chapter 39. (Isn't the ostrich in 39:13–18 a comical creature?) What does this animal-focused chapter add to our understanding of the Lord?

✦ The Lord ends his first speech with a final question for Job, one meant to rebuke Job for being a "faultfinder" (40:1), for blaming God for his suffering. Now, having listened to the Lord, what does Job vow to do in 40:4–5?

2. WHAT ABOUT EVIL? (40:6–41:34)

God comes to Job a second time out of the whirlwind (40:6) with the same instructions as the first time: "Dress for action like a man; I will question you, and you make it known to me" (40:7). For most of the book, Job has sat with his friends questioning the goodness and fairness of God, but the Lord is turning the tables on Job. As Job listens—as he gets his eyes off himself and onto God—his perspective is beginning to change.

✦ Of what does the Lord accuse Job in 40:8?

✦ What does the Lord say to Job in 40:9–14 to humble Job's heart and thereby change his thinking?

Evil is something that serves God's purposes,
not only in Job's life but in our lives too.

✦ In 40:15–24 the Lord describes Behemoth, a powerful creature. The word *behemoth* is actually a plural word (meaning "more than one") for some sort of large farm animal.[28] What impression do you get of this Behemoth?

The Lord turns Job's attention from the Behemoth to another mighty creature, Leviathan, in 41:1–34. An entire chapter of Job is devoted to this creature.

✦ Describe your impression of Leviathan from 41:1–9.

✦ The Lord describes Leviathan in 41:1–9, and then, using Leviathan as his basis for comparison, what point does the Lord make about himself in 41:10–11?

✦ As you read more about this fierce Leviathan in 41:12–34, what characteristics in particular make it more frightening than any other creature?

Leviathan

Leviathan in biblical imagery is the archenemy of God, the prince of the power of evil, Satan, the god of this world (as Jesus calls him), the one who holds the power of death. And in the Leviathan we see the embodiment of beastliness, of terror, of undiluted evil.[29]

✦ How does Revelation 12:7–9 help us understand this Leviathan?

"Maturity is the ability to carry the unanswered question in faith, holding to the Word by which we live. . . . Is it more important to me to understand than to obey?"[30]

✛ Mighty power—both the Lord's power and Leviathan's—is put on display in Job 41, but the Lord's speech had depths that were hidden from Job. How wonderful that those depths aren't hidden from us! How are those depths revealed in Colossians 2:13–15?

The Lord's description of Leviathan brings the book full circle. The Lord created Leviathan, and he is able to defeat the creature he created. Just so, Satan was allowed to attack Job, but only under the limits and authority established by God. And here is where we find one of the biggest takeaways of the book—evil is something that serves God's purposes, not only in Job's life but in our lives too. And this realization—that God is all-knowing, all-powerful, all-wise, completely just, and so totally sovereign over everything, including evil—is what leads Job to humble repentance.

> *"Our answers to evil and suffering tend to focus on trusting God in dark times, on waiting for our lives to get better, on God's working all things out for good, and on the hope of heaven. These answers are certainly not wrong. God's answer to Job, however, is entirely different: he affirms the utter goodness of the world Job has been criticizing. . . . Trusting in God's final defeat of evil, and remaining mindful of the war being fought over us, gives us strength to endure in our relationship with God while he allows Leviathan some measure of power over us."*[31]

LET'S TALK

1. How do you pray when you are suffering? Do you address God as though you had a right to an explanation? Discuss how we can pour out our perplexities to God with total honesty without crossing the line into ungodly demands or ultimatums.

....

....

....

....

....

2. God stuns Job—and us—with the fact that he controls not only all the good things that happen, but also the evil things. We understand that animals kill and eat other animals because of the fall—all killing and bloodshed is the result of human sin. But God tells Job that not only does God allow such killing; he himself sends prey to bloodthirsty animals (39:26–30). Discuss why the Lord's hand in and over the evil things that happen can be a source of comfort rather than fear.

....

....

....

....

....

....

....

PEACE AT LAST—AND PROSPERITY TOO

JOB 42:1-17

At long last, Job is at peace. As we begin this final week in our study, Job's circumstances haven't changed—not yet. Even so, he's at peace because God has come and revealed himself to Job with powerful words. Job hasn't learned the reasons for his suffering, but that's okay. The Lord has made himself known to Job, and that's enough. And all along, isn't that what Job has wanted most of all? Job has learned, and, as we will see, accepted, that the Lord God governs every detail of creation, including the painful, evil tragedies that afflicted Job—and those that afflict us too. Job is at peace because he sees God now, and what he sees is power and majesty and wisdom. But God isn't finished with Job yet. He is about to reveal even more of who he is and what he does in the lives of his people.

1. TURNAROUND (42:1-6)

The Lord has finished speaking, and we see from Job's response just how deeply the Lord's words have impacted him.

✦ How does Job's declaration in 42:2 demonstrate real faith?

✦ The Puritan Thomas Watson defined repentance this way: "Repentance is a grace of God's Spirit whereby a sinner is inwardly humbled and visibly reformed."[32] Where in Job's words in 42:2–6 do we see these indicators of true repentance?

Job declares, "I had heard of you by the hearing of the ear, but now my eye sees you" (42:5). What a powerful testimony! In today's terms, Job is saying that as a result of his suffering, his relationship with God has moved from his head to his heart. Before his great losses, he'd believed in God—his power and ability to bless. But Job's suffering has created such a deep yearning to understand and know God that when God finally answers, Job's heart has been sufficiently tenderized to really listen. And as a result of listening with spiritually enhanced ears, he is able to see with the eyes of his heart.

> *"Where we might wish to argue that omnipotence ought to have stamped out evil at its first appearance, God's chosen way was not to crush it out of hand but to wrestle with it; and to do so in weakness rather than in strength, through men more often than through miracles, and through costly permissions rather than through flat refusals."*[33]

2. GOD'S MERCY AND THE POWER OF PRAYER (42:7–10a)

For the first time in the entire story, the Lord directs his words—sharp words—to Job's friends Eliphaz, Bildad, and Zophar.

✦ Why, in verse 7, is the Lord angry at these three friends, and how does he characterize their speeches?

✦ How in verse 8 does the Lord deal with his anger toward the three friends, and what does this reveal about the Lord's character?

In speech after speech, Job poured out his perplexity, frustration, and often downright despair in the face of God's silence and what seemed to Job like God's injustice. But, amazingly, God says here in verse 8 that Job had spoken right things about him! How can that be? The Lord's earlier rebuke of Job (38:2; 40:2, 8) shows us that Job certainly wasn't sinless in all he said. What we see here is how deeply the Lord cares about Job's heart—despite Job's bitter words, he never lost his desire to know God and be known by him.

✦ The Lord instructs Job to pray for Eliphaz, Bildad, and Zophar. If you think about how these friends treated Job during his darkest hours, such prayer was no small thing. Yet Job's restoration is linked to this prayer for his friends—the Lord made this prayer the turning point in Job's life. What does all this reveal about the Lord's heart for relationships?

3. TWICE AS MUCH (42:10b-17)

As we near the final verses in this lengthy book, we see Job's life turn around in dramatic ways. In fact, not only does the Lord restore all Job lost—he gave Job twice as much as he'd had before.

✦ One of those happily-ever-after scenes is set out for us in verse 11. Scenes like this typically happen only in Hallmark movies, but this one is for real. How does verse 11 reverse Job 19:13–15?

....

....

....

....

✦ When we talk about something being double or twice as much, we're often speaking figuratively: "This batch of cookies is twice as good as the last batch," or "Let's skip the movie and go to the beach. It'll be double the fun." But when we're told that the Lord gave Job twice as much as he'd had before, it's meant literally. It's no figure of speech. Note the specifics in the chart below.

	Job 1:3	Job 42:12
Sheep		
Camels		
Oxen		
Donkeys		

✤ Before tragedy struck his life, Job had enjoyed family life with seven sons and three daughters. Look back at 1:4–5. What do you see there about the father heart of Job?

In light of what we see back there in 1:4–5, the sudden, shocking death of all ten was surely a big reason for Job's declaration shortly after his losses: "The thing that I fear comes upon me, and what I dread befalls me" (3:25). Job had the same desire that all godly parents have, that their children will walk with the Lord and be numbered among his people for eternity. With the death of his kids, Job would never have any assurance about their spiritual well-being. But here, at the end of the story, we get hints of something absolutely amazing.

> *"Behold, we consider those blessed who remained*
> *steadfast. You have heard of the steadfastness of Job,*
> *and you have seen the purpose of the Lord, how the*
> *Lord is compassionate and merciful." (James 5:11)*

In 42:12 we see that the farm animals Job lost were restored exactly double. But then, in 42:13, the doubling pattern seems to be broken. Job tragically lost ten children, and here he receives ten new children—seven new sons and three new daughters. But that's not double, right? It's the same number of kids as he had originally. According to the pattern, he should have been given twenty new kids—to replace the original ten. Yet why should we assume the pattern is broken? If the pattern holds, Job does have twenty children now—ten who are alive and ten who, although dead, yet live. We might have here one of the earliest hints in Scripture of the resurrection. If so, if that is indeed the case and the doubling pattern holds with the children, it might be that the Lord was answering the pain in Job's father heart, giving him the assurance he thought was lost forever. We don't know for sure, but it certainly would reflect all that the Lord has revealed of himself to Job—author of life and death, ruler of creation, all-wise, compassionate, and faithful.

At the beginning of the story, we see the father heart of Job; here at the end, we see the father heart of God. He hears his people's prayers for their children. After all, he understands firsthand what it means to lose a son. Unlike Job, who would have done anything possible to spare the lives of his children, God willingly gave up his own child in order to save ours. "For God so loved the world, that he gave his only Son, that whoever believes in him should not perish but have eternal life" (John 3:16). Yes, God has compassion for parents. He knows parent angst and parent grief. Jesus himself, in his final dying hour on the cross, took note of his mother Mary and her agony in losing him to such a horrible, violent death. So great was his compassion, even in his darkest hour, that he reached out to provide for her, knitting together his mother and best friend John in a family bond (John 19:26).

✦ We never knew the names of Job's children who died in the storm, and we aren't told much about his seven new sons here at the end. The focus is on the three daughters. What are we told about these girls in 42:14–15?

....

....

....

....

....

> *The book of "Job is passionately and profoundly about Jesus, whom Job foreshadows both in his blamelessness and in his perseverance through undeserved suffering. As the blameless believer par excellence, Jesus fulfills Job."*[34]

✦ In what specific ways do the reversals in Job's life continue up until his death?

....

....

LET'S TALK

1. Job's losses weren't restored until after he'd prayed for his friends—the very ones who had harmed him. What does this reveal about the Lord and what matters to him, and how might it reshape the way you currently pray, and those you pray for?

2. Job's change of heart is pretty dramatic, and it was the Lord's words that changed him. Think about how the Lord addressed Job—not only the things he revealed about himself and his ways, but also his gentle use of questions. What does this reveal about how the Lord leads us to repentance also?

....

....

....

3. As we come to the end of Job, note what you've learned or what's affected you most about:

   · the character of God:

....

....

....

....

....

....

....

....

....

....

....

   · the way of salvation:

....

....

....

....

....

· the path of discipleship:

HELPFUL RESOURCES
FOR STUDYING JOB

Ash, Christopher. *Trusting God in the Darkness: A Guide to Understanding the Book of Job.* Wheaton, IL: Crossway, 2021.

Ash, Christopher. *Job: The Wisdom of the Cross.* Preaching the Word. Wheaton, IL: Crossway, 2014.

Kidner, Derek. *The Wisdom of Proverbs, Job, and Ecclesiastes: An Introduction to Wisdom Literature.* Downers Grove, IL: InterVarsity Press, 1985.

Ortlund, Eric. *Job: A 12-Week Study.* Knowing the Bible. Edited by J. I. Packer and Dane C. Ortlund. Wheaton, IL: Crossway, 2017.

Piper, John. "Which Characters in Job Can We Trust?" Interview. Desiring God website, June 19, 2020. https://www.desiringgod.org/.

NOTES

1. Christopher Ash, *Trusting God in the Darkness: A Guide to Understanding the Book of Job* (Wheaton, IL: Crossway, 2021), 140.
2. Graham A. Cole, *Against the Darkness: The Doctrine of Angels, Satan, and Demons*, Foundations of Evangelical Theology, ed. John S. Feinberg (Wheaton, IL: Crossway, 2019), 108–9.
3. Eric Ortlund, *Job: A 12-Week Study*, Knowing the Bible, ed. J. I. Packer and Dane C. Ortlund (Wheaton, IL: Crossway, 2017), 16.
4. Christopher Ash, *Job: The Wisdom of the Cross*, Preaching the Word (Wheaton, IL: Crossway, 2014), 21.
5. "Lament for Saul and Jonathan," Ligonier, May 24, 2019, https://www.ligonier.org.
6. Ash, *Job*, 83.
7. "Job's First Lament," Ligonier, June 3, 2015, https://www.ligonier.org.
8. "Did You Know? What Is Sheol?" in ESV® Student Study Bible (Wheaton, IL: Crossway, 2011), 654.
9. Ash, *Trusting God in the Darkness*, 37.
10. Adapted from Ash, *Job*, 101–2.
11. Ortlund, *Job*, 33.
12. As a follow-up, you might want to check out Nancy Guthrie's book *What Grieving People Wish You Knew about What Really Helps (and What Really Hurts)* (Wheaton, IL: Crossway, 2016).
13. Merriam-Webster, s.v. "foreshadow," accessed May 3, 2022, https://www.merriam-webster.com.
14. Ash, *Job*, 226.
15. Derek Thomas, "God's Sovereignty and Glory," Ligonier, April 1, 2022, https://www.ligonier.org.
16. Ash, *Job*, 260.
17. ESV® Study Bible (Wheaton, IL: Crossway, 2008), note on Job 25:1–6.
18. Ash, *Job*, 262

19. If you want to learn more about your conscience and how it functions, a good resource is Andrew David Naselli and J. D. Crowley, *Conscience: What It Is, How to Train It, and Loving Those Who Differ* (Wheaton, IL: Crossway, 2016).

20. R. C. Sproul, "The Book of Job," Ligonier, February 1, 2007, https://www.ligonier.org.

21. David J. Reimer, "Introduction to the Poetic and Wisdom Literature," in ESV® Study Bible, 866.

22. Ash, *Job*, 284.

23. Ash, *Job*, 305.

24. John Piper, "Job: Rebuked in Suffering," Desiring God, July 21, 1985, https://www .desiringgod.org.

25. John Piper, "Let the Young Speak," Desiring God, August 29, 1982, https://www.desiring god.org.

26. Ash, *Job*, 375.

27. Ash, *Job*, 393–94.

28. Ash, *Job*, 410.

29. Ash, *Job*, 421.

30. Elisabeth Elliot, *Discipline: The Glad Surrender* (Grand Rapids, MI: Revell, 1982), 70–71.

31. Ortlund, *Job*, 78–79.

32. Thomas Watson, *Doctrine of Repentance*, Monergism, accessed June 20, 2020, https://www .monergism.com.

33. Derek Kidner, *The Wisdom of Proverbs, Job, and Ecclesiastes: An Introduction to Wisdom Literature* (Downers Grove, IL: InterVarsity Press, 1985), 59.

34. Ash, *Job*, 436.

Flourish Bible Study Series